HOW TO EARN YOUR LIVING
FROM THE THINGS YOU
LOVE TO DO

MAKE YOUR
CREATIVITY PAY

PETE MOSLEY

Who is this book for?

'This book is for everyone out there that has a head full of ideas and the notion that earning a living from their own creative endeavour is simply the best thing ever.'

It's aimed at:

- People with a hobby on the verge of a business - working from home, studio or garden shed.

- People who are desperate to escape the 9-5, or through redundancy or change of circumstances, need to start afresh.

- Start-ups and fledgling businesses needing ideas, inspiration, and a guide to what works.

- More mature businesses that need some fresh thinking

- Folk who are looking for a friendly, jargon free guide

People like you:

Wood-turners, glass artists, potters, cake-makers, furniture makers, artists, coracle-builders, soap and candle makers, calligraphers and illustrators, jewellers, bead workers, blacksmiths, spoon carvers, knitters and weavers, model makers, leather workers, basket makers, toy makers, musical instrument makers, rug makers, well - all creative people!

If you recognise yourself in this list, Make Your Creativity Pay will resonate, because for you it may well fill a need, solve a problem, answer questions, provide help and support, get you heading in the right direction.

It will help you 'Make Your Creativity Pay'.

Published by:

PSB Design & Print Consultants Limited:

PO Box 5, Driffield YO25 8JD

Registered Office 38 Salisbury Road, Worthing, West Sussex BN11 1RD

Registered Number 1613161 - VAT Registered Number 371185455

ISBN number 978-1-873847-01-5

First Edition published 2011

Acknowledgements

This book has been produced in partnership with craft&design magazine. I'm really grateful to Paul and Angie, who have given me support and encouragement throughout.

I'd like to thank Anne Currie – proofreader extraordinaire, for making sure i's were dotted, t's were crossed, and that the odd lapses into non-standard English – i.e. Glaswegian, were kept to a minimum.

I'd also like to thank the other members of the craft&design team – Jan, Mike and Rachael for help and support along the way.

Thanks also to Wayne - at dv8design.co.uk - who designed my beautiful cover.

And I should really acknowledge my local, The Beacon Inn, for the regular use of a quiet corner to stroke my beard and think and write.

Dedication

I'd like to thank my partner Janet, whose innate creativity inspires me on a daily basis. Her keen eye for repetition, hesitation and deviation has been a godsend. And my son Felix who read an early draft and said 'it's really good'.

My brother Frank and my father have been pivotal too – their adventures, trials and tribulations in self-employment informed my mindset as I grew up. It's in the genes. And my Mum's indomitable spirit needs to be experienced to be believed. These people made me who I am.

Thank you

Foreword

This book is for everyone out there who has a head full of ideas and the notion that earning a living from their own creative endeavour would be the best thing ever. From my point of view creative endeavour takes in a pretty wide swathe of human activity. In truth, the mere fact that you already have or are seriously considering starting up a small business based on your own skills and ideas guarantees that you fall within my definition of creative. And being your own boss beats the pants off 9-5 any day of the year.

The contents of this book - the reflections, observations and insights, are informed by literally hundreds of conversations with people like you over a long period of time. In that time I've seen some brilliant ideas executed and some real doofers which predictably ran aground. What I've realised is that there are a few underpinning immutable truths about making a business out of one's innate creativity. Adhering to them seems to make the difference between success and failure.

So - why write a book like this when there are so many small business guides around already? Well, partly because so few of the books are truly aimed at creative people - it's as if there's a bit of a clash of language and world view going on between people who make and do stuff and the world of mainstream business advice. My own coaching and mentoring work is designed to bridge that gap. Indeed, business development organisations often employ me to provide that support precisely because, over time, I have accrued some pretty unique experience in the field of profitably combining creativity and small business models.

Like a lot of creative people, my academic career stuttered along in its early stages. It took me a couple of shots to get the right combination of qualifications I needed to go to Art College. My very first creative job was at Govancroft Potteries in Glasgow (a major manufacturer of stoneware whisky flagons) - they had a nice little studio where I threw wonky pots for the gift shop - it prepared me well. After graduating, I started my career proper as Town Artist in Chorley, Lancashire in 1979, then moved to Leicester to head up a new arts facility for unemployed 16-25 year olds in the City Centre where we ran workshops in Visual Arts, Photography, Music and Drama. In 1984, I started my own company, delivering arts workshops in education and community settings – schools, hospitals, community centres, prisons, and day centres. I also forged a link with an Arts in Education company in New York and spent many summers working in the States throughout the 80's.

I've been working for myself ever since - making, doing, training, problem solving - increasingly by working with other creative people who want to get their own small ventures off the ground. I also write about it – I'm

Business Editor for craft&design magazine and write both online and offline content for them.

I specialise in coaching and mentoring creative and exceptional people – helping them start and develop their creative businesses.

You won't find much jargon in here or too many technical terms, but you will find those immutable truths I mentioned that have helped me to run a small business and advise others through thick and thin for all these years. As you'll discover, it's the tough times that help you acquire and keep your cutting edge.

"Whatever you can do, or dream you can, begin it. Boldness has genius, magic, and power in it. Begin it now." Goethe.

Contents

The Fire in Your Belly

So. You're curious about the business of being creative, and you've decided to do something about it. Maybe you've already started.

Have you got the fire in your belly? By that I mean the combination of fear and excitement that you'll need to drive this project of yours forward to the point where money starts going into your bank account by dint of your own ideas and efforts. Have you got what it takes? Have you got the tenacity and self-discipline you need, both to start and to keep going? Because you're going to need a healthy measure of all of these things if you are to succeed. Creativity, skills and talent alone will not guarantee the success that you crave. Nor will the kind and supportive words of friends and relatives – in fact you need to beware of those very things.

Are you – despite your excitement, fear and anticipation – putting off the actions you need to take to commit to this path? Do you seem to be a long time in the preparatory stages? Yes? Don't worry, this is a healthy sign. This is resistance at play – and the degree of resistance you put in the way of getting on with making the dream a reality is a sure sign that it is indeed, exactly what you need to do.

Read, research, above all talk to people, prepare, become informed – do what you can to allay your worries and trepidations. But finally it comes down to this – decisions, followed by action. Stoke the fire.

Why Do You Do What You Do?

It's important to be mindful of your motivation - because we are not all motivated by the same things. You need to know what fuels your fire, and seek out plentiful supplies.

What satisfies you more - recognition and financial reward, or the pure joy of creation? Or do you walk (like most of us) a bit of a tightrope between the two? Do you find the rigour of working to commission, or mass producing 'bread and butter' artefacts exciting, or does this dull your senses and blunt your creative edge?

As a business mentor, I regularly meet with clients who are frustrated by their inability to earn all of their living from their creative activity, or what they do earn isn't quite enough to fund the lifestyle they might aspire to.

People get round this in all sorts of ways – I met an artist the other day who worked as a full time fireman in the hope that the 4 days on, 4 days off rota might give both enough money and regular and useful slots of time to meet his creative goals. Traditionally creative people have always taught, run workshops and demonstrations or held other part time jobs in order to make up the shortfall. I've met many that have learned trades or taken up new skills like website design as a second string to the bow.

But when you come to weigh up the need for income versus job satisfaction, where does it leave you?

The inbuilt problem for creative people is that they are motivated more by intrinsic factors - the love of what they do, the creative muse, the magic of it all coming together - and less by extrinsic factors like money and material rewards. In fact, scientific surveys of creative activity show that whilst quality remains high when working on projects that have been commissioned by others, levels of creativity drop. The focus on monetary reward coupled with the external influence of the commissioner on the idea itself can suppress the magic.

There are also other issues in play – creative people choose the self-employed lifestyle because it also gives them autonomy – freedom to live as they wish, and the time to master, by constantly practising and improving, the craft of their choice. It's a brave decision, often challenged at various points by parents, family or friends. These challenges alone often make the difference between sticking with it, or not.

So how do you reconcile freedom of expression with the need to put food on the table? A large number of successful creative people get a large proportion of their income from secondary sources - which all sounds a bit bleak. But let's think about the science again. If the creative edge is indeed dulled by monetary rewards, what's so wrong with earning at least some of your income in other ways?

The clincher for me is this - the people who consistently do the work they love in an uncompromised way, and as a result create works of quality that are imbued with authenticity and passion, usually end up harvesting richer rewards than those who doggedly try to link the monetary reward directly to the creativity.

Clearly, one shouldn't bankrupt oneself and one's family creating and trying to sell work that doesn't cut the mustard, and I acknowledge that it's sometimes hard to see whether your work is or isn't of sufficient quality to make the grade. However, I do regularly see great people with considerable potential giving up because of the money vs. creativity struggle – and that's a shame.

So what am I really getting at?

The first thing, I think, is not to beat yourself up if your creative output doesn't immediately create 100% of your desired income stream.

Second, in terms of personal satisfaction, having a clear purpose within your work is probably more important than the financial reward. People who choose to work towards those intrinsic, value laden goals are less stressed out and more satisfied than people who chase money all the time.

Third, having an occupation where, at least part of the time, you are master of your own destiny and where you get to work with and learn about what you truly love – and where you are in a state of flow more often than not - beats the hell out of working full time for someone else.

Fourth, the trickiest bit is finding and balancing the things that will earn you the money with the things that you really love to do but which may never earn you a fortune.

Fifth, if you are already able to combine all of these things and have the lifestyle you always dreamed of, you are lucky or gifted or have worked extremely hard – probably a bit of all three.

The truth is, most of the truly successful people I know have worked extremely hard. I knew someone who had worked for the Moscow State Circus who said this, 'If you want to excel (in your chosen craft) you must work 25 hours a day - you must steal an hour each day from your death'. The subtlety of this, I'm sure, is lost in translation - but it didn't stop the message hitting home.

I'm not going to try and provide an answer here - every single person I work with resolves this in different ways. But the realisation that the work that you do for money and the work that you do for love can be separate things is healthy and can actually free you up in a quite significant way.

If you find yourself spending more time pondering on all

this stuff than you feel is healthy, it pays to take some time out to compare notes. Find someone who is achieving the things you want to achieve and go and ask them how they have done it. It's very rare that someone will refuse to share a bit of wisdom. I explore ways of doing this in more detail later in the book.

The Stuff of Survival 3

The ideas I introduce in this chapter are things that I wish someone had taken me aside and thrashed into me when I first started out. Life would have been a hell of a lot easier. In a sense, they are the immutable truths, basic rules that really should be followed. The paragraphs that follow summarise the main themes that will be explored in detail as we move through the book.

I've worked with lots of creative businesses, and have evaluated and assessed many more. For all of that, I reckon success in most areas of business boils down to a small number of really simple factors. Get these right and most other things fall into place. What I say here applies equally to painters and mosaic artists, musicians and cake makers. The same rules apply right across the spectrum of micro-enterprise.

Do your research

Whatever you do, don't go into this venture blind. Scour the web to see what your fellow entrepreneurs are doing. Go to popular shopping areas – especially the ones that have clusters of the specialist shops or outlets you'd like to sell to. They've not appeared there by accident. Read, talk to people, attend events. Look at other people's marketing materials. Get to know the marketplace inside out before you begin. If you don't do this, how can you expect to be a skilled player within it?

Quality - of your ideas and products

In the end, success boils down to having a product or service that people want to buy. That people will buy in sufficient quantity to sustain you. So it's got to be good.

Please don't commit to starting up until you are convinced that this is the case. Be objective, check it out with people who can give neutral feedback. Pay attention to the feedback, and refine your ideas as necessary. Skip this step at your peril.

Supply and demand

I often visit colleges and talk to arts and humanities students. When the subject of self-employment comes up the most common fear that comes into people's minds is the spectre of having to deal with record keeping, the taxman, banking and accountants.

I always feel that this is approaching the problem from the wrong end. The real issue when starting a small business is to do with supply and demand – you need to know for sure that there's a big enough demand for your product in order for you to cover all your costs and for you to make a decent living out of it. Finding out about the other stuff is relatively easy in comparison to figuring this out.

Know your market

Study your niche. Can you identify and list all the different types of people who will buy your product? Do you understand their wants and needs? Have you asked them? Will what you make and do fulfil their dreams and desires?

Will people be eager to buy what you make or do? How will you know? How can you find out?

Quality – in your dealings with others

People pay more for quality. This is true. But it will really help you along if you infuse quality through everything you do – not simply in terms of what you produce. Don't rush, take your time, pay attention to detail on every level. Great presentation counts for a lot, but nothing impresses people more than having someone take the time to make sure everything is 'just so'. Every one of us can define great customer service – far fewer actually deliver it. Get this right and everything else will be easier.

Building track record

Get known for doing a great job every time. Be consistent. Ask your customers what they want. Ask them how they want to be treated. Ask them how they'd like you to communicate with them – and how often. Ask them to tell you if you make a mistake or fall short of their expectations. If you do – don't justify it – apologise and never make the same mistake again. Build your track record and reputation systematically, record everything you do. If you are just starting out, student committee experience, volunteering, work experience and internships count too. Good references and testimonials of any sort count.

High quality documentation

Get a good camera and learn how to use it well. There are excellent workshops you can attend to find out how to capture great images without spending a fortune on professional photography. If you get the chance to have professional photos done too, grab the opportunity when you can. It's more about having a representative selection of great, well lit shots than having dozens of moderately good ones.

If video is appropriate, for instance to capture the excitement of a piece being made or performed, or to explain a unique process, then find a way of getting the video too. And don't forget to put it on your website or blog.

Whenever someone says something positive about what you do, capture it – write it down, record it, video it – whatever you need to capture it for posterity. Collect press cuttings, and don't be afraid to ask for quotes and testimonials. If people like you and your work they will give these freely.

Superb communications

Think about a business or individual that has really impressed you recently. The chances are that a large part of the impression they have made on you comes down to the quality of the dialogue you have had with them. Politeness, patience, promptness of response. Did they listen carefully to your request, and answer the question you posed, rather than trotting out a carefully rehearsed corporate pitch? Great communications differentiate a great business from a merely good one.

Talk to your competitors – they might actually be your allies

I'm always amazed by how cagey people are about their perceived competitors. Scared I guess that others will grab their share of the market. To use an analogy – if you are shopping for shoes, where would you rather go? To a local village with one shoe shop, or to a city where you know there are many shoe shops within striking distance of each other?

Big retailers use this clustering phenomenon to their advantage. The lesson to be learned here is one of differentiation. If your work stands out you will have nothing to fear from being in proximity to, or even working with, your competitors.

Find the gatekeepers and befriend them

People who run small businesses find themselves being encouraged to network all the time. That's fine, but you can spend a lot of time talking to people who have also gone to the networking event to sell, not buy. Also, very few of us are natural networkers – it can be an uncomfortable and unrewarding activity. By far the best strategy is to take time doing a bit of forensic research to work out who the gatekeepers really are. By gatekeepers I mean people who have influence or decision making power, and who probably already know all the other contacts you are trying to find.

Find the gatekeepers and expend your efforts on building a relationship with them – preferably in advance of asking them for their advice or help. Build on any common ground you find. Then show your hand and ask for the help you need. I can't stress enough that success depends on building first class relationships with people.

Get some feedback

One of the very first things to do is to get a thorough appraisal of your work – from as many viewpoints as possible. If you are a student, you will be used to hearing the views of your peers and tutors. This is not the same thing, I'm afraid, as bravely putting your work in front of potential customers out in the real world. Don't rely on Ma, Pa, mate or partner to tell you whether your output cuts the mustard. You need to know the ugly truth.

Without that feedback, you don't get the information you need to fine tune your creative output to the needs of the marketplace.

It's often a good idea to test the water in small ways first. By that I mean trying to sell some of your products before formally committing to starting a business. Start by talking to family and friends – do a bit of 'mates' marketing. Let them know what you are trying to do.

See if there are any social opportunities for you to show your work to people and give them the opportunity to buy it. You can also try things like approaching local traders or even going to local community fairs just to engage with a lot more people and see if they are interested enough in the things that you make or do to buy them.

Geography and critical mass

Geography is a critical factor. Where do you want to live and work? It's worth opening up a large scale map of your region and thinking about the following things:

How many cities and towns – large population centres – are within striking distance? List them. Draw a circle on the map that delineates a comfortable travelling distance – to visit retailers to encourage them to take your work and later, to deliver stock to them. Do some research. How many shops and other potential outlets are there within your chosen area? In marketing terms, is there a big enough slice of your target market close enough to you so that you can both make and sell effectively in the time you have available?

If you are going to supplement your making with teaching or workshopping, you need to think about all the places that might be available to you for that portion of income too.

Baby steps

The appeal of starting out small and growing in small

increments is that you lessen the risk. The truth of the matter is that it's a minority who make a full time living straight away, and those who do tend to be mature businesses that have been building up turnover over a number of years.

By building the business up over time it lessens the need for huge amounts of startup capital, and allows you to make informed decisions about when to move to the next stage.

A lot of people dive straight into starting a small business and invest large sums of money on equipment, stocks of materials, perhaps even renting studio or retail premises before they have really tested the market. It's a worrying statistic, but around a third of small businesses fail within the first three years. This happens for a number of reasons – usually because people fail to check out the actual demand for their product before they start the business in the first place, or because they don't take account of the real costs of running the business and the cash-flow difficulties those costs can create.

Take advice – and then some more – and then again

Use experts in areas where you are clearly not expert yourself. In areas such as taxation, book-keeping and accountancy, it's very easy to think that by doing your own tax returns, self assessment etc., that you will somehow save yourself loads of money. The truth is, an accountant will spot everything you can legitimately claim, and will save you much more than the cost of their fee each year. A good book-keeper will also save you money by presenting your finances in a format that your accountant will find easy to read and interpret. The less time it takes for your accountant to read your accounts, the less you will have to pay them.

Don't be afraid of the taxman

For some reason, people develop a huge fear of dealing with the tax office. I have to say, in my experience, they generally bend over backwards to be helpful, as long as you play by the rules. Most tax offices run advice sessions, surgeries and workshops for start-ups. The tax office websites are very helpful, with loads of advice on what to do at each stage of getting started, in relation to tax and national insurance.

Tackle problems early

Lastly, if you run into difficulties, ask for help. Struggling away on your own might feel heroic, but it seldom solves the problem. A bit of timely advice can work wonders – and often others can think of solutions that you have missed. And if the situation is bad, a bit of moral support goes a long way.

Nurturing Relationships

4

It's all about relationships. Everything. All your marketing efforts boil down to one thing - getting warm human beings to say 'yes' to your proposition. And it's these relationships, once built, that will sustain you through good times and bad.

People buy from people. People buy when they sense there's a shared value system, or shared world view, or a shared aesthetic. In short, when they feel they have something in common with you. Values are important. Projecting your values within your story could be one of the most important things you ever do.

For example, if you work in environmentally friendly ways, advocate fair trade or use only ethically sourced materials, you need to tell people. If there is a strong social or spiritual theme within your work, it's a valuable part of your story. Be clear and open about these things.

In order to maximise your chances of success there are three things that you need to ensure. Your work must be of sufficient quality for people to want you to come and work for them again and again, you must develop and maintain a personal 'Track Record' which proves you can deliver on your promises, and you need a clear sense of your values. These things will enable you to communicate key aspects of your work with clarity and conviction.

If you work hard to maintain all of the above, you will probably find that after a while work begins to come to you as a result of personal recommendation. This is the most effective form of marketing you can possibly employ. Ideally, you want people to be contacting you with sales enquiries or interesting opportunities rather than you having to endlessly send letters or publicity leaflets to people to try and stimulate their interest. It takes time to establish this pattern – but the initial effort involved could well set you up for the rest of your career. So – what do you need to do to make this happen?

Essentially, you need to focus on the way that you build relationships. It's all about creating and maintaining relationships with key people in your field. This is best achieved by communicating wisely and effectively rather than by employing scattergun marketing techniques such as huge mailings of letters and leaflets or employing indiscriminate email campaigns. People will only hate you for doing this.

To do this well, you first need to build a complete picture of the network that exists within your field. You then need to identify key people, organisations and companies within this who will be the starting points for your own personal network.

The best way to start this process off is to grab a really large sheet of paper and start to visually map out the people and organisations that you know about and have some contact with. Use lines to connect people and organisations that you know are connected in some way – you will be able to use these existing networks and relationships to help get your message across. Ask others to help you with this -- especially more experienced people who can point out bits that you have missed or that you have been unsure about including.

The 80/20 rule

Getting a large part (80%) of your business from a relatively small proportion (20%) of your clients is regarded as the norm. So it makes sense to secure your relationship with the 20%. Talk to them, give them a bit of extra attention, throw in the odd freebie or a bit of extra time. Keeping them is often all about the quality of relationship you maintain with them. However, and this is the big one, circumstances beyond your control can take these customers or clients away no matter how good the relationship.

Therefore it pays to be constantly on the lookout for and developing relationships with potential clients who have the same sort of profile as your existing 20%. Widen the gene pool. Make relationships with potential customers even if it might be ages before you actually get a contract from them. Always look for people who are equivalent in some way to the folk you work with already. Make friends with them and cultivate them. It's a good insurance policy. Oh, and by the way, when you lose a client, don't throw away the personal relationship. Cultivate that too, as you never know when an old contact might bring new business back in your direction.

The real trick is to use your network in a way that cuts out the need for 'cold calling', or gets other people to help make the difficult introductions.

If you do want to send something in the post or by email, here's how to make sure people read it:

Getting people to read your mail is problematic at the best of times. Getting them to both read it and respond to it is even harder.

The basic trick is this: Never, ever, send anything to anyone unless you have spoken to them first.

Think about how you sort your mail in the morning - junk mail gets binned, brown envelopes go in the 'pending' pile (unless they are cheques - you'll be looking out for those!), and business and personal letters are put in different piles.

Then, before anything else, you always open the post that you have been waiting for with a sense of anticipation. The sense of anticipation is usually underpinned by a business or personal relationship.

So, in order to make sure your mail is not only opened but prioritised:

- Talk to the person you want to send stuff to.

- Ask them for guidance on the format of your enquiry, application, or the service they want to hear about.

- Customise the mailing to their requirements.

- Call them, or email, and let them know that the letter is on the way.

- Use a first class stamp, and put it in the mail.

This also works with documents you want to send digitally.

Of course, this only applies to one-off or very small mailings. It does, however, help build the relationship.

Finally, if you get what you need, say thank you for the help and advice. Next time you write they will remember you and treat you as someone with whom they already have a working relationship.

Why it Makes Sense to Ask for Help

5

When you work alone, isolation can really sap your motivation.

It's completely normal to run into situations where you don't know the answer, or become paralysed by seemingly conflicting options. When you think this is happening, it's time to ask for help. And the process of finding help can have some really exciting spin-offs.

Our instincts tell us to beware of rejection, and yes, it's not a very pleasant experience. However – for every person that refuses to help you, there will be many who will willingly share their experience with you – and it's a rare situation where someone, somewhere, has not experienced and overcome precisely the problem you seem to be stuck with.

There are four or more potential outcomes from a request for help:

- An outright rejection – rare, but possible.

- A genuine attempt to help, or at least signpost you to someone more qualified.

- The beginning of a new and fruitful working relationship or networking opportunity.

- Serendipity puts you in exactly the right place to not only solve the problem, but change up a gear at the same time.

Years ago, I developed a creative workshop which I wanted to sell to schools. It worked, but only to a limited degree. Someone I met socially handed me the business card of a company in New York who specialised in running creative education workshops. One evening, whilst feeling a bit down, I drafted a letter to them, asking if they could recommend a solution to my problem. A few days later, I got a call from the director. He invited me to go and work with them for three weeks – they would provide accommodation and advice, if I could raise the airfare. Needless to say, I jumped at the chance. I learned everything I needed to know at the time and gained a working relationship that lasted for years, with me returning to New York many times to work and visit my new friends.

The truth is, you never know when, where or how the next break will come, so remain open to opportunity and ask for help when you need it.

Even the most experienced of us needs help and advice from time to time. We all suffer from two big blocks when it comes to promoting ourselves; a threshold of anxiety that we must cross when dealing with anything or anyone new, and a whole range of self-limiting beliefs that we can only conquer by talking them through and watching carefully how other people have overcome them.

Ask people you know to point out who else you might talk to – and ask if you can mention their name when doing so. This establishes credibility, and increases the chance of your message being listened to.

Seek advice from the best possible sources – other people who have already experienced the ups and downs of getting started. The more successful someone is, the more likely they are to have asked for help themselves along the way. Be brave and contact people you admire. Tell them why you particularly want their help – because you like their work perhaps, or are fascinated by the way their business has developed.

Seek out professional networks and groups that might help. There are lots of them around, and a web search will turn up a whole range of options. Asking around will turn up many more.

Above all, don't try and do it all on your own. One of the strongest trends of the last couple of years is the move towards collaborative production and marketing. Who could you team up with to make your offer stronger and share the effort and risk?

Coaching, Mentoring and Creativity

6

Top level professionals in every realm of sport and business use coaching to improve their performance, solve problems and set clear goals. Most of us recognise the value of a coach in those contexts. We are often less clear how a coach might engage with us as creative people. In truth we are probably more used to artists engaging with 'mentors'. So what's the difference, if any, and how can a coach or mentor help get us where we want to go?

Let's start by demystifying the definitions themselves – and we are going to find that in most respects, the practices of coaching and mentoring overlap so much that the terms become almost interchangeable.

Both coaching and mentoring will provide advice, guidance, support, encouragement and challenge to another person. Within this range they can be used in a variety of contexts. These contexts can range from pastoral care to career development, from creative development to simply broadening horizons. However, they work in very different ways.

Here's some history

In the Oxford English Dictionary a 'mentor' is defined as a wise or trusted adviser or guide. The word originates from the tale in Greek Mythology when Ulysses, before setting out on his epic voyage, entrusted the care and development of his son Telemachus to his old friend, Mentor. Mentor was entrusted with being caretaker of the kingdom, and these duties included helping the young Telemachus to prepare himself as a future ruler. He was encouraged by Mentor to think for himself.

A mentor is someone who can be a long-term guide, counsellor and friend and one whose insights are valued thus providing a positive role model for the person. A mentor can help guide someone through an important transition in learning, they can help that person to come to terms with a new situation, or work on possible career development and creative growth.

A coach, on the other hand, approaches things differently. Coaching is a relationship which is designed and defined in an agreement between a client and a coach. It is based on the client's expressed interests, goals, and objectives.

The coach may use inquiry, reflection, requests and discussion to help clients identify personal and/or business goals and develop strategies, relationships and action plans intended to achieve those goals. Clients are responsible for their own achievements and success.

The client takes action. The coach may assist, but never leads or does more than the client.

In my experience, if you want advice about your creative practice, tools, techniques and materials, a mentor who is a more experienced practitioner tends to work best. If you need help with motivation, strategy and goal setting or you suffer from dreadful procrastination or artist's block, a coach is more likely to have the background in psychology that's required to tackle these things.

The best of these supportive relationships develop within well matched pairs who work together to find their own way through the process, rather than pairs who are tied down by too rigid targets and timescales. For this to happen, a coach or mentor needs to be a highly skilled and intuitive individual, well chosen and well matched to the client.

Regular business advisers often struggle to be accepted by creative people as there's a lack of common vocabulary and a different map of the world at play. Most creative people do understand that there are rules that are common to all businesses, but find it easier to talk about the business of creativity with someone who also comes from a creative background.

A creative professional who provides support in a coaching or mentoring style can help precisely because they understand just how closely life and the creative muse are intertwined.

The power of coaching is that it works with people and their businesses simultaneously, in a very synergistic way - energising, removing blocks, and clarifying goals, enabling people to articulate their ambitions.

Finding a coach or mentor

Knowing what you want from your coach or mentor can make it easier to decide where to go to find the support. There are three mains ways of accessing support:

Business mentoring schemes

These are designed primarily to help you develop your business. Mentors are trained specifically to work in that area. Most will come from a business background, and they are encouraged to help the client look at the business in the round, taking into account work/life balance as well as the bottom line. These are usually hosted and run in conjunction with business incubator spaces, but can be applied to by firms within their geographic catchment area.

Arts and crafts specific mentoring

At any given time there are usually a number of arts-specific schemes in operation. It's always worth checking regularly with your Arts Council, Crafts Council or your own regional network of support to see what's available in your area. A Google search for 'artists mentoring scheme' will bring up at least half a dozen articles about recent and current programmes of support.

Working with an independent coach or mentor

I've found that a fair number of people prefer to avoid mentoring schemes, choosing instead to work with an independent coach. The benefit of this is that there is no external agenda influencing the flow of the work – the only targets to be met are those set by coach and coachee as the work progresses.

You also get to choose the place, timing and duration of your meetings. Some people like their support in short bursts, and others like to draw down support over a much longer period of time.

The nature of the support is more flexible. The focus can change as required from business and marketing through to more personal issues to do with overall career progression, changes of direction and whole life goals, work/life balance, personal fulfilment or stress and energy levels.

Coaching is also a great way to tackle the myriad things that get in the way of progress – procrastination, perfectionism, self-doubt, and fear of presenting in public – to name just a few.

A lot of the people I work with are dealing simultaneously with two or three of the following issues:

- Creative block

- Stalled career

- Creativity vs. pressure to earn

- Discomfort with requirements of funders/grant givers/commissioners

- Energy depletion

- Disorganisation/lack of a plan

- Negativity/lack of self esteem

- Need for a 'creative catalyst'

- Help with marketing and profile

- Developing and taking advantage of supportive networks

If you've never had a coach or mentor, it can be a liberating experience. Independent coaches should always offer you a free diagnostic phone call on a no obligation basis. I would recommend talking to a few before making a decision – you are after all interviewing someone for a very important job.

Your Niche, Your Expertise

7

You need to know what your niche is - in other words, what's the unique area you want to work in? Once you've nailed that, make sure people appreciate the level of expertise you have. Then you're in a stronger position to make the most of your unique qualities. But how do you do this, exactly?

Before spending a fortune on marketing, get to understand your values. What is your creative DNA, the thing or things that people really love about what you do? Know what differentiates you.

There are four stages to this:

● Understand your niche, your product or proposition.

● Find a way for people to discover and taste or sample your product in some way. Gather feedback; get endorsements and positive comments - especially from individuals that are from your target group. Create advocates who will help you spread the brand. How can people find and sample your product? This is 'discovery' marketing.

● Incorporate this feedback into your marketing. Don't spend large amounts on marketing until you are sure that all of the above elements are working. As soon as you know something is working - immediately scale up or increase your effort in that area.

- Be clear about who it is that you want to buy from you. Target carefully - it needs to be laser precision marketing, not scattergun.

Repeat this process with new ideas or products. Tell your story in slightly different ways for your different audiences.

Positioning yourself as an expert means you can charge more (or at least as much as you can) for your product. What does that mean? It's not charging more for the sake of it – it's charging more because it is unique and distinctive and it resonates with people's higher sense of value.

Who are your customers now? What is it that they are buying into? How do you make your niche bigger? Who else is a bit like the people you already sell to?

Stand up and be counted

I'm convinced that creative people need to acknowledge their own expertise more, and harness the benefits that come from sharing it with others. I've set out a few simple steps which will help you establish a high profile and use it in ways that your customers, friends and colleagues can share and enjoy. And the added bonus is this – get it right and it will boost your sales, too.

Most of us tend not to regard ourselves as experts, and maybe even shrug in a self-deprecating way when someone else makes a really complimentary comment about our work. The odd thing is that we can all easily identify an expert or two in our field – individuals who are simply much more experienced, talented or inspired than we regard ourselves to be.

Think about this. Who do experts look up to? They do exactly what we do – they too identify people that they feel are more experienced, talented or inspired than they are. And so it goes on.

So why then even think about positioning ourselves as a specialist in our field?

People gravitate towards specialists who connect with their needs at the right level at any given time – an expert who knows their audience, what they need, and how to connect with them.

There will always be people who know more than you, and people who know less than you. Aspire to learn from those with more knowledge, and pass on your learning to those with less.

Be someone who isn't afraid of saying, 'Yes! I have knowledge to share'.

Someone qualifies as an expert when they consistently:

- Help others achieve results.

- Solve problems.

- Know and can explain how they do these things.

- Keep learning from others who know more and share their increasing level of knowledge as part of a continuum.

Raise your profile – use your unique skills and knowledge

One of the questions I am asked most frequently is this: 'How can I raise my profile, establish my credibility, and become known more widely for what I do?'

If this is what you want, then it is essential to do the following things. You don't need to do them all in the same place at the same time, although you can use your website to show these things to good advantage.

- Showcase the things you've achieved in life and work. Be proud of the experience you have and don't be afraid to share it with others. Give up the reluctance to stick your head over the parapet.

- Show your qualifications (if you have them), they are important. Your CV and website should list your qualifications, experience and any masterclasses or courses you have attended. If you have public and/or product liability insurance, professional certification or evidence of good character, let people know – it builds your credibility.

- Be visible, be known, have a reputation for being a specialist. Hiding away doesn't do anyone any good at all. Who do you want to be known by, and for what? Brand yourself as the person that people seek out for these things.

- Share success stories, facts, figures and testimonials. Tell the story of your life and work – broadcast this where you can.

- Use publicity. Give talks, workshops and demonstrations of your skills and knowledge. Appear in public. Speak up at meetings. This doesn't need to be complex – people will be interested.

- Write articles, put 'How To' sections on your website or blog, be open to sharing what you know a lot about.

- Tell people about the things you make or do. Explain techniques, materials, processes – how the thing you are selling was made. Customers love to talk about the things they buy, so the more you can tell them, the better. A product factsheet that tells the story of the article is a neat way to do this.

- Keep learning about the things you are passionate about – not so you know the most (unless that's what appeals to you), but enough to understand the territory of a particular audience, and to use your knowledge to inspire people.

- Distil your knowledge down to 'bite size' chunks of

information. People will respect you if you give small amounts of high quality information at any given time. Hone it down to fundamentals – distil your wisdom like a fine scotch whisky.

- Aim to be friendly and approachable.

I'm guessing that you will be able to tick at least some of the boxes straight away, and that you are already displaying some expert attributes.

Defining Your Portfolio 8

Portfolio working is simply a term that applies when you make your income from providing more than one product or service. It's very rare to offer only one thing, and in evolutionary terms, it's dangerous too. In the next three chapters, I explore a range of options that you may wish to consider.

One of the benefits of doing the job I do is that you get to speak to lots of people with small creative businesses. Over time that adds up to a huge number of different viewpoints on the world. It allows me to gauge really carefully what it is that people want. It also allows me to gauge really carefully what people like you are doing in response.

I've worked with some big hitters, people who are working, exhibiting and selling their work internationally. Even the ones who are working on a big scale often have other sources of income. In effect, most folk have a portfolio of products and things that they do. I think it's worth taking some time to think about what having a portfolio means.

How a portfolio develops

Most small scale entrepreneurs think in terms of having

a product or service. They develop that to the best of their abilities and go on to earn some cash from it. They put all of their efforts into making their product or service visible to as many people as possible.

At a certain stage, people then start thinking about teaching - they regard themselves as having enough experience or expertise and at least the basic skill-set and communication skills required to go out and teach other people how to do it. So the 'how to' workshop, either in the educational domain, or open to the public, or indeed open to other artists and artisans, becomes a really valuable second string to the bow. Then, usually, that is followed by the realisation that people are interested in listening to your stories.

After that it doesn't take long to progress to the stage where you may wish to talk, lecture or demonstrate around your area of expertise, and that's the third part of the portfolio.

When I first started out on the freelance trail, I persuaded my full-time employer to let me go part-time. I then had a little bit of security - a base from which to explore my ideas and test them out. The testing phase (essential market research in my view) enables you to find out what does and doesn't work and lessens the chance of coming a cropper. I ended up marketing two different workshops to a wide range of venues, doing a little bit of lecturing, and keeping my very part time job for the first few months. It just seemed to grow naturally from there, and as time passed I left my part-time paid employment behind and slipped into full-time self employment without taking any huge risks.

Many creative people find a similar synergy between a number of activities to create dynamic, meaningful and profitable combinations.

I know a great number of creative people who make work, teach others about their art form, and give 'expert' demonstrations and talks about their subject. That's a common model. But lots of us add other, different, elements into the mix.

There are just as many different ways of portfolio working as there are creative people around, it seems - it's a huge and varied list. I know this because I surveyed exactly this activity recently, and was amazed by the results. For example, some were:

- Teaching, lecturing or running workshops

- Undertaking repair and restoration work

- Doing paid work in a non-arts field

- Working in arts administration or event management

- In part-time employment

- Running a gallery, a shop, or were involved in retail

- Hosting painting, crafts or writing holidays

- Combining making with further studies

- Relying on pensions, or had property, B&B or rental income

- Organising their own fairs or exhibitions

- Running party activities for both adults and children

That's just a small selection from the whole sample.

The nice thing is this - there's no 'normal' in this respect. If it works, you can do what you like - but I stress the 'if it works' bit.

The next three chapters concentrate on the three main elements of a traditional portfolio - making and doing stuff, teaching and workshopping, and talks, demonstrations and writing.

Portfolio 1
Selling the Things You Create

9

Sell by every appropriate means you can. The key word here is 'appropriate'.

You need to identify your route to market, and figure out really carefully where you want to focus your efforts. This will enable you to use both your time and your budget effectively.

Find out how other creative people are doing this

Look very carefully at everybody out there who is selling products or services like yours. It doesn't matter whether that's ceramics, top end jewellery, wooden toys or willow caskets.

The rules around this are fluid and people are using interesting blends of different sales and marketing techniques, both on and offline, to get where they want to go.

First things first:

What I would really encourage you to do is look at other people's websites, blogs and Facebook pages, and above all not to be shy of going and talking to other people who are doing something similar or who are already in the part of the marketplace that you want to get into. They will tell you what works. Don't be tempted to skimp on this stage.

Check what your customers want, and what they are prepared to pay

Equally crucial is the process of gauging demand for your product, and what people will be prepared to pay for it.

The interesting thing is that the process of market research - of finding out what people want and what price they are prepared to pay - can also be used to find out their preferred channels of communication - that is, how they'd like you to be in touch with them.

So you need to get out there and ask people - but how do you do that? You can't be roving around the countryside all the time. The quick answer is to use an online tool like survey monkey or twitter survey, or to use your email list to send out a short questionnaire to people.

The funny thing is this - about half the folk you will email really like doing surveys! It's an interesting phenomenon - they send you the answers back. The answers you get to your surveys (providing you ask the right questions) will give you a huge amount of information. You can then proceed knowing you've taken the necessary steps to ensure that you are selling the right thing to the right people at the right price. It's really reassuring to have that information and feedback.

At every possible opportunity, ask questions. When folk ring you up, or get in touch via your website or blog, ask them the question - where did you find out about me? You'll find some patterns in the answers which will help you target your message more effectively in the future.

There's only one way to ensure your marketing mix is right, and that is to continually ask people what works for them. If you're not asking the questions, you can't expect to stay on the ball.

Are you a maker or a do-er? Or a bit of both?

How you answer this question will affect how you choose to do your marketing. One message will not do for everybody. If you produce things for sale and run workshops, for instance, you may need to get a couple of complementary streams of marketing activity going. These things almost always need to be sold in different ways. Think about it from your customer's point of view – what do they need to hear, see, touch or experience to help them choose your product?

If you mainly make stuff, you need to:

Get your product on show - literally and metaphorically. Make sure it's going in front of the right people - be discriminating. Scattering it all over the place can be a huge waste of effort.

How and where could you put this across?

You say:

- This is what I make

- This where you can find it, touch it, fall in love with it

- This is what other customers have said (quotes)

- This is how you can buy it

If you mainly do stuff, you need to:

Show how what you do solves problems, i.e. focus on the benefits to the buyer. If you're going to run a workshop in a school it needs to have a clear understandable outcome. The simplest way to do this is to tell your version of this story:

'I/we do this, with these people, and as a result of doing that, this happens, and I/we know it happens because the participants tell us this, and independent observers tell us it works too, and we have the stories and case studies to prove it.'

How and where could you put this across?

You say:

- This is what I do

- This is who I do it with

As a result of doing it, these things happen:

- For the venue (school, community group, youth club)

- For the participants (describe them)

We know this is true because:

- Someone who took part told us (quote)

- Someone who paid for it told us (quote)

- This is where you can find out more.

A quick exercise

Here's a challenge: try to write a personalised version of those bullet points, for one or both strands of work, on one sheet of paper per strand. Keep it simple and to the point.

Now - where will customers get to buy your stuff?

Get a big sheet of paper, ask a friend or two to help, and map out the answers to these questions:

- Where do you go to buy nice things?

- Where might your customers go to buy your things?

- Where do they go for inspiration?

- Where do they go to learn about things, do classes, attend talks and lectures?

- Where might they socialise and network?

Go as broad as you can with this exercise. Your answers should cover both online and real world activity. Be as divergent and creative with your answers as you like.

Think about places that resonate with your values, likes and dislikes – funnily enough, your ideal customers are likely to share some of these.

The chapters entitled 'Telling your Story' and 'Connecting Traditionally' explore the specific techniques you can use to carry this message across.

Portfolio 2 Teaching and Workshopping

10

The thing about teaching and workshopping is that you get the chance to work with people and share your skills. If you've got the inkling that you'd like to do that, it can be a marvellous experience. There's nothing quite like being in the flow when you are running a workshop. Apart from anything else, you learn a tremendous amount from the people you're working with. This can be a great source of inspiration.

You may be starting from scratch. You may have been thinking about adult education classes or teaching at a local college, or maybe you're already doing those things and thinking about how you can extend them. Either way, the first step to starting or extending your work in this area is to make sure you have documented everything that you have done thus far brilliantly well, and have written an outline of the way your activity works. You can then use this to get a conversation going with the people you'd like to work for.

Where can you do this?

The truth is - anywhere you can imagine getting a group

of interested people together. The opportunities are astonishing in scope. I have personally worked in schools, colleges, universities, youth and community centres, hospitals, prisons, young offenders and probation services, day care centres, residential homes for the elderly, Women's Institute groups, arts and craft studio groups, galleries, Air Force bases, church groups, Scout groups, upstairs rooms in pubs, in the back of a transit van, in tents, at festivals, in fields and on playschemes. All have their own unique challenges.

Do stuff for free (but just the once)

If you are starting out, a great way to build a track record, test ideas and gather feedback is to do something for free. For example, if you imagine you'd like to run workshops, find someone who wants something similar and offer to run a session for them – but on the strict understanding that they will help you document the session and allow you to evaluate what happens as a way of gathering feedback, comments and testimonials. This is also an opportunity to have someone take some photos. Then you can use everything you gather to put together a publicity pack that shows clearly that you can deliver a great experience that everyone will enjoy.

If you haven't yet run a workshop, then there are some really simple ways to approach that and test it out, and get some cracking documentation and feedback at the same time. This could be as simple as gathering a small group around your kitchen table, and sharing what you do. Friends and family are not bad guinea pigs when it comes to this.

I can remember running a session round my kitchen table doing some fused glass, years ago, and it was just such a fun way of finding out what did and didn't work. People brought cameras and took really nice images that they were prepared to share because they'd had fun. They wrote some brilliant comments to support my new idea because they liked what they had done and what they took away at the end of the session.

It's not that hard to make a start and it's only a small leap from there to finding a friendly face at a local school or community venue that might be prepared for you to come and do a more professionalised version of the same thing. When you've hit that stage you should then have all the material and the confidence you need to market it more widely.

Testing ideas in more depth

All the planning in the world won't save you if something is wrong with the basic premise of your idea – so what do you do?

It pays to test out your ideas in a relatively safe environment – you may not be sure how long certain things might take, or how a group of a certain age or ability range might react to the basic idea.

If you search around, you ought to be able to find an environment similar to the one you want to use the finished idea in, and someone in charge who is happy to let you experiment. You needn't try and run the whole thing through – maybe just arrange to do a couple of short sessions where you can gauge reactions, whilst still giving the group a decent experience. If you don't give the group something tangible, the test won't work and you won't get invited back.

You can use this set-up to test out different styles of personal presentation, ways of working with groups, arranging your equipment, experimenting with ways of working with different age ranges, etc. Let the host know what it is you are trying to resolve, and they will probably be happy to talk it through with you, especially if they feel it will ensure that the group enjoys the session and gets something worthwhile out of it.

On another level, what you are involved in here is a subtle PR exercise, and a way of getting free publicity material. Sit down at the end of the session and do some evaluation with them.

If you are dealing with younger children, get them to do a drawing and write a few words about what they have done. With teens and adults, a question and answer session and a 'comments' sheet will do the trick. Be prepared to get both positive and negative feedback, and treat it like the Holy Grail. Feedback is power – it lets you know what you are getting right, and what to discard or amend. Use this feedback process properly, and it will help you develop both the content and your own presentation skills. Ask any other adult observers to write some comments down for you. Or, as I did, get into the habit of carrying a digital memo recorder with you, and do mini interviews. This will then provide you with photos and comments to build into future publicity.

Depending on how eager you are to promote yourself, you might like to repeat this process in other venues around your patch. You might feel you are running short workshops for no material return, but you will be building a reputation for caring about the quality of your work, and involving hosts and organisers etc., in the process. This will count for a lot later on.

Once you feel you are ready, you can start marketing the idea with confidence, knowing it's a good, well researched and tested product.

Assessing your group

Every group you work with will throw unique challenges your way, so you need to be prepared for all sorts of contingencies and happy accidents. It is possible to reduce the chance of disaster striking if you gather information about your group in advance from whoever is normally responsible for the group, or by going and meeting the group yourself.

Talk to the group leader well in advance of the session – try to glean as much information from them about the group as you can.

Don't be afraid of asking very direct questions. The answers you get will be coloured by the host's perception of the group, and may not be totally objective, so dig around a bit.

These are the sorts of things you might need to ask about:

● Have the group done anything like this before – are they used to working with creative people?

● Prior knowledge and experience – do they know anything about the activity? At what level are they likely to engage with it?

● What level of curiosity/desire to be involved are they likely to display – are they there by choice?

● What sort of presentations are they used to – formal assemblies, informal group presentations, large or small groups?

● Age range and cognitive development.

● Concentration span.

● General behaviour – quiet and receptive, or noisy and chaotic?

● Level of familiarity with tools and materials – how much time will you have to spend on familiarisation and practice?

● Level of manual and mental dexterity.

● Are there any restrictions on things they can use, e.g. will they try to eat it? Use it as a weapon? Steal it? Scissors, sharp knives, staple guns etc., are barred in some institutions.

● Where are they used to working – in classrooms at desks, or in the hall, on the floor?

● Cultural or religious considerations – do you need to exercise sensitivity in terms of language, appropriateness of activity, photographic documentation etc.?

Even after thorough checking, it's often wise to build in an appropriate introductory activity that will give you the chance to gauge the group for yourself – something that will let you judge level of maturity, attentiveness, the sort of language they will accept – all the things that tell you how to 'pitch' your presentation.

Remember this: every single person that comes to one of your events becomes an advocate for you and your work. If you can give them a little pack or a card or a goodie bag to take away at the end of the day then every session has a multiplier effect. Most sessions will provide you with some recommendations or referrals.

There are two strands to this. The first is the session itself and the income you earn from it, the second is the power of it to extend people's understanding of you and your story. There's a really good marketing opportunity built into every event you run.

Portfolio 3 Talks and Demonstrations

11

The third portfolio option is to start speaking about or demonstrating your craft. In certain contexts you may also be given the chance to sell work or publications at the same event.

Content

What can you speak about? As a practitioner you need to focus on things that you love - that way your passion will come through and people will really connect with what you are talking about.

Makers and do-ers have a distinct advantage when it comes to public speaking. Because, as a creative person who is making unique things, plucking ideas out of thin air, you are by nature one of the most interesting, absorbing and fascinating people on the planet. You must remember that, and don't forget that the more interesting your demonstration or imagery, the less you need to say.

So - what is your area of expertise? That's your starting point.

Presentation tips

Avoid 'text only' powerpoint presentations like the plague. If you can demonstrate something, that's brilliant. If you must illustrate your talk with slides then use mainly visuals. If you can, mix in some video. It's much better to have a sideshow that's driven by visuals or interesting activity and talk over the top.

To maintain interest you need to present a mix of talk, visuals and involving input. It's good to get people to think about things or participate in some way, even if that's just good old questions and answers. If you say you welcome questions at any point, or at the end, you'll get plenty of them.

Overcoming anxieties

There are a number of ways you can ease yourself into public speaking without exposing yourself to massive embarrassment or dropping a cog in front of a big audience by trying to do big stuff before you are ready. Hold in mind the notion that people love to hear stories and think about small scale local opportunities to have a bash at this.

I would recommend seeking out a local speakers' club, attending a couple of sessions, sitting in the back row, just to see how things are done. Or if there's a PechaKucha night somewhere (20 slides/20 seconds per slide) go along to that. These are ideal ways for you to gauge for yourself the level that people start from. You may well be gratified. You might find out that you are better at talking and presenting than you thought.

If you can't talk for twenty seconds about a slide of your work, I'd be surprised. You may already have a number of images that you could talk about for 20 seconds - so build your presentation up from there. You don't need a PechaKucha night to do this - you could do it for a local group, or at a business networking breakfast. It's a nice simple format and you can use it anywhere.

Maybe the notion of speaking at a business networking event fills you with dread, but it's actually a harmless way of getting into public speaking for the first time - and maybe for the first time to an audience of people wearing suits. That's always an interesting experience. In comparison to what they will usually be listening to, you will be a breath of fresh air, believe me, and they'll be on your side. And you wouldn't believe how bad some business people are at presenting. Oh yes.

Doing it is the easiest way to overcome the fear, and having done it you may find it's one of the most exciting things you've ever done. Thereafter, it just becomes a breeze, and you'll be actively seeking out opportunities to speak.

An opportunity for sales

We've all experienced talks and presentations where you realise that all you're getting is a thinly disguised sales pitch. It's easy to leave an event like that feeling you've been slightly cheated.

There's something to learn from that. Some of the best talks, presentations and training sessions that I have been to have involved no selling whatsoever. There was nothing on a table to buy, no overt marketing message during the programme.

But what has happened is that the speaker has injected their presentation with energy, has stimulated curiosity and interest in their audience and has asked and answered questions, thereby building real rapport.

Those are the presentations where you go up to the speaker at the end of the session and ask her for a business card or contact details. Those are the ones that are likely to generate business, book sales or referrals.

If you've got some wonderful work or a book, by all means take it along and put it on a table at the back. Where you need to exercise sensitivity is in the extent to which you use the opportunity as a blatant sales pitch. It's the feeling of being 'sold to' that blunts the authenticity and warmth of the experience. The whole thing is perceived differently.

It's the relationship that counts, and the quality of the conversation that people will remember. If you look on it as a chance to start a relationship with a group of people, over time those relationships will be worth much more to you than the sales you make at the back of the room.

Places to speak

You can often find opportunities to speak at: Women's

Institutes, libraries, schools, sixth form colleges, local bookshops, universities, Rotary Clubs, Round Tables, Lions Clubs, galleries, business networking groups, studio groups, business incubators, Chambers of Commerce. In truth it's a list that's only bounded by imagination. If you want to talk to non-arty audiences, your accountant or bank manager or doctor or dentist may well point you in the right direction.

Portfolio 4
Ready Reckoning

12

Once you have decided what the various parts of your portfolio are likely to be, you need to decide what proportion of your available time you will spend on each. This in turn will dictate how much income you can expect from each part.

Here's a handy technique you can use to help you find the right balance of income earning and creative activity. I use this on a regular basis with clients, and it usually helps them visualise how to divide their time effectively.

It also helps with the very important issue of setting financial goals – which are critical. You need to be able to estimate your inflow and outflow of cash as accurately as possible.

The process can be divided up and tackled in number of easy steps:

1. Decide how many days a year you are available for work. Don't forget to take into account any days of paid work you do for other people.

Start with 365, then subtract weekends (or if you work weekends, the weekday equivalent thereof). Subtract the number of 'holiday days' you wish to take. Then subtract the number of days you need to spend on admin, marketing and running your business. Think about and subtract the number of days you might estimate to be ill each year. Finally think of the number of days you might want to devote to things which may earn you no money at all – reading and research perhaps – or being a parent or carer. And then take off any days that you will be working for someone else.

How many days are left out of 365? Whatever goal you have set yourself for self-employed income will need to be earned in that number of days.

2. How many different things do you do (or plan to do) which will earn you money?

For some, this will be simple:

- Making

- Teaching

- Online trading

For others, more complex:

- Making

- Running workshops

- Working as guest lecturer

- Working part time for an arts organisation

- Selling designs

Whatever they are, list them all.

3. Take a large sheet of paper. Draw a pie chart that shows roughly what proportion of your available days you will spend on each activity. The pie chart approach lets you visualise the proportions easily.

On the list or in each 'slice' of the pie chart, write down the number of days you want to devote to each.

Now, bearing in mind the total income you want in the coming year, how much can you reasonably charge for a day's activity in each area of work? Do the sums. At this stage, this will usually need careful thought and adjustment. You should end up with a balance of activity that lets you hit or exceed your financial goal. Don't forget that your total must cover all your business costs, tax and NI that you will have to pay, and your personal drawings.

If it doesn't, check that your pricing is realistic, i.e. properly pitched, in each area of work. It can pay to compare notes with other people if you are at all unsure about what you might be able to charge for particular activities.

You may need to increase or decrease the number of days you have allocated to certain things.

Planning ahead in this way puts you in control. When you have established how many days' work you want to get in each area, you can begin to assess how to go about your marketing. You can then allocate your time and budget accordingly.

Telling Your Story 13

We know that more and more people are buying original contemporary work and choosing to spend their disposable income on hand made one-offs rather than chain store 'me-too' products.

Why is this?

When a customer buys something from an artist or artisan they are buying much more than an object. They are buying into a set of values. They are buying something to beautify their home or adorn themselves, and they will also be hoping that their friends and family will appreciate and share their taste and their 'eye' for design. There's a certain amount of unabashed one-upmanship in owning something truly unique.

The people they show their purchase to will have questions. Usually questions like 'Where did you get that?' 'What's it made of?' 'How's it made?' And crucially – 'who made it?' So you really need to supply the answers to these questions.

If you know these questions are being asked, how can you turn this mutual appreciation of the finer things in life to your advantage? In truth, the answer is simple. Make the story, of both the object and your part in its making, into part of your daily conversation with customers old and new. By sharing the story, you increase the perceived value of the work – they are not just buying an object, they are also buying a tale to share with their friends – of the object, and of its making and maker. And then, if friends and family really like what they see and hear, they will probably start looking out for something like it for themselves.

It's a no-brainer, really. So where, when and how do you tell this tale?

Here's how to get your story across:

Engaging with customers at events and shows

Very few people are comfortable selling face to face. You do however love what you do! If you focus on telling the story, it can make the process of selling much more comfortable – you are simply sharing information about what you do and how you do it. In many cases, if you do this, the sale will take care of itself.

Traditional marketing – brochures, postcards, display materials

These are usually used to carry images of the work. However, that's only part of the message – it needs to be a balance of both pictures and the story of the product and the 'how' of the pieces.

Talks and Demonstrations

Although these are often delivered to a small audience, they are one of the most powerful ways of getting your story across. People who attend these events go on to talk to others and carry the story forward on your behalf, especially if you've got a story-based card, brochure or handout to give them.

Website content and downloads

Your website offers all sorts of opportunities to tell your story - it's not just the 'About Me' page either. Short videos of the making process, of your studio interiors, of you talking about what inspires you, all add to the customer experience – remember they take this away and talk about it. They are far more likely to pass on links to a website or blog that has interesting content like this.

Social media

Every time you post on Twitter or Facebook, embed a link to an image, a video, or an article about your own work, or your specialist craft. Don't sell overtly (although some do this effectively by tweeting a link to the latest item they have posted up on Etsy.com). Rely on the story and interesting content to get people coming back.

In conclusion

By far the most powerful use of these tools is in the telling of your creative stories.

The most effective way to make friends, build relationships, gather support, find collaborators, win over the doubters, sway opinion and - dare I say it, sell your wares - is to tell your story. Don't be shy. Tell it loud and clear. People will read it, watch it, listen to it - because as a creative person who is making and creating all the time, you occupy the position of being one of the most interesting, absorbing and fascinating people on the planet.

Surprisingly, I often find that really hard to get over to people when I'm running seminars or speaking at conferences. People ask me all the time 'will people really be interested in what I have to say?', or 'will a magazine or newspaper editor really attach much importance to what I'm saying?'

The truthful answer is that you are going to be much more interesting to them than the vast majority of the folk that are writing to them. You are the source of good copy, you are the source of great stories, and you are the source of powerful visual material and interesting content that they just won't get anywhere else.

In truth you make their lives much easier for them - so don't be shy about getting in touch with them.

Your audience is waiting. Tell your story – and tell it well.

Using the Internet 14

There are still a significant number of creative people who are quite wary of the Internet as a marketing tool, despite strong proof that it really can raise your profile and, over time, send a steady stream of new and returning customers to your door. Part of this, I have to say, is a healthy concern about the amount of time it takes to maintain an effective web presence.

I'm going to split this section between exploring why you should use the Internet and how you should use it. Sounds a bit obvious, I know, but the Internet is evolving exponentially, and nothing should be taken for granted. It's a very different place now from the place it was when I first joined up in the 80's. It used to be all about email and websites, and it stayed that way for a while. Then it started changing.

The web is becoming a place where you can get close to people, talk to them and listen to them carefully and build relationships with them. That's why it's becoming such powerful tool for you to get your message across.

This section looks at aspects of web marketing: websites, blogs, social networking, the use of email as a marketing tool, and how traditional marketing can work alongside and support your web based marketing efforts. I'll try and explain how you can use these things effectively without having to expend a huge amount of your valuable time. I'd also like to reassure you that you're not inadequate if you don't blog every day, tweet every hour or if you post to Facebook less than once a week.

Websites

Some people would say that a website is really nothing more than a glorified business card or brochure. In some respects I have to agree with that. It's like an online shop window where people can come and inspect your wares. There are others who say the only reason to have a website is to collect email addresses to build your mailing list. You can then communicate with people on a more personal level with emails that are targeted to their interests. This also can be true and I explore that further in the section on email marketing.

There are others who regard the traditional webpage as a dinosaur and who say that the world of blogs and social networking has taken over. If you look at the statistics relating to web usage globally, social networking and video have completely overtaken websites in terms of the overall volume of web traffic.

If you don't currently have a website, there are some compelling reasons to get one. It alters the size of your potential market radically, at a stroke. Anyone, anywhere on the planet, can see your work. You can post your CV, track record and testimonials up there too.

It's no longer a frighteningly expensive exercise. You can get a professional designer to make you a basic site with text and a gallery, for a few hundred pounds. For a bit more, you can have a site with 'content management' built in, meaning you can update it yourself. Or you can use a free online website service to make one yourself. It's a brilliant way to present your portfolio, even if you don't want to sell online.

A significant number of creative people have really beautiful websites with great images and descriptions of their work, but which attract few visitors and ultimately, few customers. A smaller number have sites that are visited regularly and through which they build strong relationships with the people to whom they sell their work.

This proves that superb visual design alone won't automatically ensure that your website gets loads of visitors. Nor will it ensure that the visitors you do get will actually be interested in what you are selling or promoting. What makes the difference?

There are a couple of factors at play here. First, people may simply not know the site exists and second, search engines such as Google are not directing people towards it. I'll explain how you can deal with that later in this chapter.

Make sure that you have an engaging 'About Me' page - it's often the most visited page on a site. Don't be shy, tell people about yourself and why you love doing what you do. And you must put your email button and phone number prominently on every page. Your contact details must be really easy to find.

Should I sell from my own website?

The first question you need to answer here is 'Do enough people know about my site (yet) to justify the time and expense of adding and maintaining a shopping cart or Paypal button and then updating it regularly?'

If you are just starting out, probably not. Test the market first. Make sure people want to buy the things you make. Look at, and perhaps join a site where people like you gather together to sell. Sites like Etsy or Artfire make this relatively easy. They are active online communities of people selling side by side, and lots of customers are already in the habit of going there. Yes, the sites take a commission, but you will gain valuable experience of selling online and will learn a lot from hanging out there.

When sales take off and your confidence grows, start selling from your own site. Then you get to keep a much bigger slice of your income.

Blogs and Blogging

Blogs are easy to build, allow for much more personal control over content and can be edited, personalised and changed on a 'do it yourself' basis. Unless you have enough knowledge to design and build your own website, a blog can be a great solution to getting a personal space set up online quickly, complete with any images, video or audio you want.

A well designed blog can be just as effective, if not more effective, than a traditional website, and you can set them up so you can navigate around them in the same way.

But, and this is the big difference, blogs are designed to be updated regularly. They were initially designed so you can use them like a diary, and the architecture of a blog makes this easy. You can post an article complete with a photo or video, from your mobile phone, from anywhere on the globe with a Wi-Fi link. This dynamism, the constant change, makes them extremely attractive to your readers, and interestingly enough, to Google.

Two of the most popular blogging platforms are Wordpress and Blogger. The basic versions, which are really very sophisticated, are free to use. There are many other platforms – it's really a matter of personal preference. You get a range of nice templates to use as an added bonus.

The blogging community is a friendly place, with lots of advice and expert tutorials on hand. It's a great platform for showing off your expertise and telling the story of the person behind the product.

Making your website or blog 'findable'

It's important that you know a little bit about how search engines work so you can then make an informed choice. You can do some work on the site yourself to make it more findable, or you can employ a specialist to help you do this. The process is called search engine optimisation (SEO), which basically just means making some changes to your site to make it more attractive to Google and other popular search engines.

Until recently all talk amongst search engine geeks was of 'keywords' and 'title tags'. These are the words, both visible (on the web page) and invisible (in the HTML programming language) that describe what your site is about. These things are still very important although search engines tend to look at the content of entire sites now. But let's concentrate on the simple stuff.

Search engines like Google scour cyberspace and gather data about all the sites on the web. This is then kept in an unimaginably huge database. During this search process, the engines look for information that allows them to index the content of each site - the key words and the titles of each page, amongst other things. So when people type in a search term, the Google algorithm compares the search with the contents of their own database and return results that seem to correspond to the words the person types into the search box.

For example, if you type 'bronze horse sculpture' into Google and look at the front pages of the top two or three sites (ignore the eBay results), you'll see the words bronze, horse and sculpture are used a lot on the front page. This is called keyword density - and it's one factor that can boost your site's rating. Just be careful not to overdo it.

The keywords, both on and off your page, the title tags (what appears on the tab of your page), the descriptions of your pages and the regularity with which you use certain descriptive words on your pages really do affect how easily your site will be found. If you can edit your own site it's worth working on this. If you can't, ask your web designer to do it for you, or attend a seminar on Search Engine Optimisation if you want to find out more. At the very least, make sure your site's URL has been submitted to Google.

Inbound links

While it's great to have an outbound links page that enables your visitors to explore the sites that you find interesting, those links do little to get your site found. The more effective tactic is to get others to link to you. These inbound links, especially if they link in from significant sites, help to move your site up the search engine rankings. Good links could well help you get onto page one of Google. How do you get great inbound links? Ask for them. Look at the site you want an inbound link from, check their policy on linking, see if they link to other people like you, and then ask. If it adds value for them, they'll link to you.

Social networking

I struggle sometimes to get people to take Facebook and Twitter seriously. I still hear hoots of derision and the 'I really don't care what someone's had for their lunch' retorts. Therein lies the problem. When a huge percentage of what arrives on our screen via social networking is, how shall I say this politely, 'low in relevance', it's not surprising that many folk are still not engaging with it. BUT - in amongst the chatter is an impressive amount of truly excellent content.

The thing we need to focus on is just how effective this truly excellent content is. It's generous, warm hearted, giving, and doesn't carry an overt marketing message. The best of it is pure and engaging storytelling.

Social networks bring us close to people - followers and friends have chosen to fall into step with us. They have willingly opted in to our stories. Share ideas, pictures, galleries, videos, podcasts or downloads - 140 characters and a well chosen link can move people into spaces they've never been before.

Not many days pass when I don't get a number of emails telling me that I have new followers on Twitter. I seem to have gone viral - albeit in a fairly modest way. It comes down to mathematics really - if you assiduously sit and follow people who share your values and interests - they follow you back - and at a certain point, their followers start following you as well. I reckon this begins to cut in when you have around 500 followers. I do this for craft&design magazine - and their Twitter following is in the thousands.

I did most of my initial work on 'following' at quiet times - for about 15 minutes a day - just before going to bed, or just after I'd got up and made a cup of tea. It takes the pain out of the process.

There's a blogger called Hugh McLeod who gives this great advice: Give a gift with each tweet - a useful link or article - don't put overt marketing messages in your tweets, and leave a trail of 'breadcrumbs' - easy to follow links back to your website, blog or Facebook page.

Video and other media

A large part of the growth in video is explained by the huge rise in people using YouTube, Vimeo and other video platforms to tell their stories. An appreciable amount of that is people like you showing work, explaining processes, and telling the story of how stuff is created.

An increasing number of people are putting both video and audio material on the web and leaving it there as part of their portfolio. They are also carefully tagging these files and linking back to their websites and blogs.

Google loves this, ranks it highly, and rewards it with higher search engine rankings. Why? Because Google likes change and dynamic content. If you are updating your website regularly, embedding video from YouTube, audio from SoundCloud, and stills from Flickr, then you are creating dynamic content that people will love to interact with and the search engines will also love.

How to use traditional marketing to drive traffic to your website

How many people do you talk to in any given week who don't really know what you do? Or what your product or service actually is? A simple postcard placed in the hand can bring colleagues, friends and casual contacts directly to your website.

If you can grab the attention of potential customers using traditional (offline) marketing materials such as postcards, business cards, flyers and brochures, they are likely to come straight to your website, bypassing all the distractions, and they will be coming because they have made a positive decision to visit. This means they are more likely to turn into customers or clients. If they see a web address on printed material, they will be curious to look at the work before ringing or emailing you, so you get an additional chance to engage their attention and impress them with your work.

You need to use every means you can to get your web address into the hands of the right people. For example:

● Business cards – to carry with you, with an image, email address and website details. It's no longer necessary to have a postal address on these.

● Postcards – high quality cards have a timeless quality about them. People often pin them on a notice board or use them as bookmarks. The reaction to these can come ages after they have been distributed, adding longevity to your marketing strategy.

● Flyers – usually printed on lighter quality paper, can

be produced much more cheaply. You can afford to distribute these in a more scattergun fashion – and it is often flyers that get included in parcels when they are delivered to clients. Flyers, because they are cheaper to produce, can be used to highlight new ranges or special offers.

● Brochures – traditionally show the full product range complete with prices and an order form. More and more people are using these as a secondary strategy these days, with the main product range on the website. They can be costly to produce and distribute. Some buyers, however, still like the 'feel' of a nice brochure.

Make sure you actively use a selection of the above to promote your website.

What else can you do?

Put your web address at the end of every letter and email you send. You can set up your email programme so it does this automatically. You can also include your logo in your 'digital signature'. It's fairly easy to do this.

Put your web address on your car or van. Signs in your office reception, gallery or workshop should invite people to your website. Print up some T-shirts with your web address and an image, and wear them whenever it is appropriate.

If someone writes an article about you make sure your web address gets included. Anyone who reads the article and is interested in what you do will almost certainly log on to your site - and this could be a very large number of people indeed.

Distribute cards every time you show your work, and always include two or three with every item you sell. If people like your work they will pass the cards on to their friends. Word of mouth is the most powerful marketing tool on earth. Someone who buys your work or enjoys your service will want to tell others about it. This peer-to-peer recommendation can be stimulated very simply by having attractive printed material to give to customers at point of sale, or included with every package you send out.

One of the benefits of this strategy is that even if customers who reach your website this way don't immediately want to buy, there is a good chance they will sign up for your email newsletter, thereby increasing the size of your customer database.

Don't forget your personal network

We all build up an informal network over the years. Our networks have within them all manner of people, from long established friends to individuals we have met just the once in passing. This network is probably much larger than the list in your email address book. It is worth working out how extensive your network really is. I'd be willing to bet that you are probably missing a few opportunities by not exploring it fully.

For example, I never used to promote my glass-making activity within my network of friends. I thought there was something vaguely dodgy about publicising myself in that way, so friends never got included when I sent out flyers. Then I thought about it more scientifically. My friends have big networks as well, for whom they are constantly buying gifts, and they often have a real headache finding things that are new, unique or innovative in some way. When I asked my friends if they would be interested in being included in my mailings, they all said yes. It would help them solve a problem. My friends also turned out to have knowledge that they could share with me about potential clients and customers that I hadn't heard about.

Using Email Newsletters

15

For a maker or do-er, the whole point of marketing is to create opportunities to make contact with people who will buy your work or services. Given that most people now have access to the Internet on a regular basis and check their email regularly, it makes sense to think about how to use email both as a way of keeping in touch with established customers and attracting new ones.

The basic rule here is to only mail people who are expecting to hear from you and who have at some point requested that you keep in touch. Randomly emailing people is absolutely out of the question if you want to maintain good relationships with potential buyers.

Opt-in email lists

Every country has pretty clear laws about what you can and can't do with customers' personal details. You must give them the choice to be added to your list as well as the option to leave it or 'unsubscribe' at any time. You mustn't give, lend, or sell their details to a third party and you must respect their privacy.

Once a customer has chosen to opt in to your list, they have effectively given you permission to mail them with reasonable regularity until such point as they ask you to stop.

I always let people know they can opt out at any time. To date, no one has ever requested removal from my list.

Newsletter options

You can send out email 'round robins' from your computer by creating a simple document with images and text. I've seen some attractive flyers made this way. There are a few major drawbacks to doing it this way. It's time consuming. It's not interactive in any way and you'll never know exactly who, if anyone, opened it. Unless they reply, of course.

Imagine sending out your emails and being able to follow exactly who opened them and how often, and which links to your website or blog they opened.

How do you do this?

You can do exactly this by using an online email platform – of which there are many. It's really easy to build your database. You can import addresses from your online address book, and you can set up custom lists to target specific messages towards. As soon as you send an email these platforms immediately start to generate reports that allow you to see what's happening. You can track every email that you've sent so you can compare how your emails perform.

You get a measure of the open rate, i.e. what percentage of recipients opened and read it, and your click rate, i.e.

who clicked on which link. This is powerful information, and it's easy to get.

Some articles and links will generate more interest than others. It's good to know what works and what doesn't, as you can then fine tune your content. There's a huge amount of online support and tutorials. You get templates to use, into which you can insert text, images, video and links. It's a wise and worthwhile investment (make sure to compare rates before signing up) and it makes your email communication look so much more professional.

How to build your email list

Provide a sheet with spaces for names and email addresses at fairs, exhibitions and shows. Encourage people who buy or browse to sign up for your e-newsletter.

Provide a contact box on your website or blog that allows people to send you a request for further information or email updates.

When you talk to customers on the phone, or answer enquiries, ask if they would like to be put on your list. Very few people say no.

You can build up a useful list very rapidly indeed, even if you only collect 20 addresses a month. A mailing list of a few hundred contacts used sensitively but regularly, can have quite an effect on customer loyalty and sales.

Do not, on any account, be tempted to pick up email addresses from websites that you have visited. This is not a legitimate way to get contacts. People will complain loudly if you do this, and rightly so.

How to use your list

Every 2 or 3 months, I set aside time for my 'pebble in the pond' e-marketing campaign. These seasonal e-fliers are very short and usually feature some update to my website or a new activity. The main purpose of the exercise is simply to remind people that I'm still around and that I'm still doing what I do. I mail a selection of people - not the whole address book, but usually folk that I haven't been in touch with for more than 3 months or so. I especially make an effort to include old clients who are still around but haven't used my services for a while.

I find this strategy more effective than blasting my whole database with e-news every month. The pebble drops in an unobtrusive way. People notice without getting annoyed, they visit my site and blog, read articles, and I often get an email back saying that they are glad I keep in touch.

The other thing that happens is that a proportion of them forward the mail to a friend, who then gets in touch and asks to be added to the list – and so it grows. Don't be afraid to say 'please feel free to forward this information to friends or colleagues'.

Don't mail people too regularly, and focus on giving information rather than demanding sales. Focus on the new - new products, new ranges, new services - our brains are attuned to notice change. Adopt a friendly tone - a personalised greeting will evoke a better response.

Target your mail

I always try to address the customer by their first name and sometimes customise the content of the newsletter so that they feel it's for them rather than a bland mail shot. This strategy can be developed further by sending out a number of different versions.

For example: one newsletter might be to clients who have bought from you before showing them things they might like to add to their collection. A second might be targeted to retailers, letting them know what is selling well. A third to individuals who have not yet bought from you, with a tempting array of affordable impulse buys.

A/B testing

When you design a new newsletter don't immediately blast it out to everyone. If it's not quite right, everyone gets the wonky version. Test it on a small number first. Better still, do what the pros do. Set up two slightly different versions - maybe with slightly different subject lines (that's what people see first in their list of incoming email). Test the two versions by sending them to smallish lists. See which gets the most opens and clicks, then send that one to everybody. This approach gives you a chance to pause, reflect and edit if required.

Calls to action

You need to tell people what to do. If you want them to go to your website, or blog, or request a brochure, give them a 'call to action' - in other words a clear instruction. If you embed an instruction like this people are more likely to follow it straight away. Otherwise they close the email and think 'I'll go there later'. Get them to act straight away. Another good trick is to write a short intro to something and finish with the words 'read more'. The words 'read more' of course, are set up as a hyperlink to the place you want them to go. Works a treat.

If you want to find out more, do a Google search for Mailchimp and Constant Contact. These two platforms are commonly used and have a good range of pricing structures. You may find others that you prefer the look of.

Connecting Traditionally

16

It's tempting, when you're just getting started, to spend substantial sums on business cards, letterheads, brochures and leaflets. It pays to think twice before doing this. If you invest in a good logo design, a matching masthead (an image file you can use at the top of letters and emails) and a nice business card, you can produce some quite convincing marketing materials on your computer.

When your income stream has grown, and you have a bigger database, you can then make a more informed decision about glossier paper based marketing materials. One caveat. Don't try to be a graphic designer if it's not one of your strengths. People will spot an amateurish logo a mile off. Don't go there.

Here are a few really inexpensive, and in some cases completely free, options for marketing your work. I've based the ideas that follow on some of the questions I'm regularly asked.

Is there a way I can co-promote with other people like me?

Contact some other people whose work you admire,

who sell to customers in the same marketplace as you – but who don't directly compete with you. For example, if you make pottery, you could team up with a cake maker. Offer to publicise their products or services to your customers in exchange for their publicising your services to their customers. It could be as simple as a reciprocal feature and links on your respective websites.

How can I use this to build my customer database?

If you are struggling to build your customer database, find someone who has the same type of customer as you and set up a deal whereby you write an article for their newsletter or blog (with a link to your newsletter sign-up box) and they do the same in yours. That way you can each grow your databases and your customers benefit from getting more choice.

How can I get more referrals?

If your suppliers and clients are happy to give you work, why not formally thank them for it. There's nothing better than getting a voucher, wine or chocolates as a thank you for referring a new client.

How do I keep customer relations sweet?

Your customers already know and trust you. It's easier to get more business from them than to get new business from somebody who never bought from you. Take advantage of this by creating some special deals just for your existing customers, and announce new products and services to them before you announce them to the general market.

It costs much much less to retain a client than it does to acquire a new one.

Reward the rainmakers

Think about and list all the people who have been instrumental in passing work your way. Craft a really sincere thank you letter and send a personalised version to them all. Not only will they be thrilled, but they will remember the fact that you took the time to do this. It will virtually guarantee that your name comes to mind first when they are thinking of someone to recommend.

Under-promise and over-deliver

Thrill your customers by adding something extra. It needn't be anything complex - deliver the goods in person now and again, throw in something new for them to look at, offer them a direct link from your website if appropriate, deliver ahead of deadline - only you will know exactly how you can add value to your customer relations.

Is there any benefit to selling gift tokens?

Everyone loves picking their own gift. If you sell products to consumers make sure you offer this option. Some people may love your stuff, but may not trust themselves to choose exactly the right gift. A token solves a big problem for these customers.

Is it okay to wear/use/flaunt my own stuff?

If you make clothing, accessories, jewellery or anything else you can carry with you on your body, you should wear it - and wear it often. Then, when you get a compliment and a "Wow, where did you get that?" next time you're out, hand them a business card! Don't forget that you are your own best sales tool and you can effectively be a walking advertisement for your own work.

Would people be interested in hearing me talk about how my work is made?

Yes, absolutely. Don't hesitate. Just do it. As often as possible.

Leading Your Brand 17

In addition to understanding the building blocks of your finances and marketing, being successful also hinges on how you present yourself to the outside world.

People are buying from you – they're not buying from a leaflet or a brochure. Yes, they'll look at those things when they're finding out about your products or to help them make a decision. But it's you and the reputation of your company that they are really putting their faith in when they get their credit card out or hand you a wedge of cash at a trade show. And if they are dissatisfied for any reason, it won't be your brochure they complain to, it'll be you.

You need to pay close attention to the way that you come across personally, and the way that you do business and interact with people.

This holds true, I think, irrespective of the size of the company. If you're a one or two person company then the leadership issue comes down entirely to you and that's both a thrilling and challenging thing and a mighty burden of responsibility.

So what can you do to make sure that you're living up to that responsibility and carrying out the tasks that you need to do really well, successfully presenting the company to the outside world, making sure that the company finances are hanging together, that the marketing is working and that there is a flow of sales coming through?

Balancing all those things together is incredibly tricky. It's even more incredibly tricky when you individually are totally responsible, not only for the creative energy and imagination that leads to the things you make and do being designed and produced and put into production, but also for them subsequently being marketed and sold.

There's a critical balance to be struck in the way you take the lead, between the internal workings of your business and the way you present it to others.

There's a technique I use when working with small businesses which helps put a focus on what's important – It's called 'Dashboard Data'. The analogy here is that running a business is a bit like flying a plane – there are loads of dials on the dashboard and they all tell you important things. Critically, there are maybe two or three that you absolutely need to pay attention to on a minute-by-minute or hour-by-hour basis. It's obvious things; have you got enough fuel to complete the journey, are you flying straight and level or are you about to stall, and have you enough altitude to clear the mountain that you are flying towards?

I won't labour the metaphor, as I'm sure you'll be thinking

already of the things that you might need to monitor within your business.

For a micro-enterprise it might be things like cash flow – what's coming in and going out this week, month or year? It might be to do with your marketing flow – are you getting the right enquiries and are those enquiries converting into sales? It might be about getting repeat sales – are people coming back to buy more? Repeat business is the lifeblood of any successful enterprise.

The challenge to you is to sit down with a pad and pen and work out what your dashboard data might be. What do you need to keep a close eye on most regularly? You will find that data to be empowering stuff.

Personal branding isn't all about the clothes you wear and the quality of your watch. In a smaller company, you are the personification of your brand. If you are a potter or a cake maker and live most of your life in an apron the chances are that folk will understand that. Okay, someone may ask you to do a talk and you may or may not wish to put on a suit or smart casuals at that point. That's both context-driven and a matter of personal choice.

It really boils down to this: the way that you talk to people and conduct yourself with others is in effect the main transmitter of your personal brand consistency.

If you have the reputation for being a cheery soul who is also exceptionally good at what they do, and who listens really carefully, and takes into account what it is that the customer really wants, then you are well on the way to creating the sort of personal brand that a creative person really needs.

However, if you're a grumpy so-and-so on Monday mornings, a suit is neither here nor there. Stay away from the phone or get someone cheery to answer it for you. I wish I were joking, but so many businesses are spoiled by a lack of awareness of the details that really count. If you're grumpy, or awkward, or you don't listen, people will simply stop calling – and you'll soon see the results in your cash flow.

At the end of the day, all marketing comes down to getting an enthusiastic 'yes!' to your proposition – whether that's a sale, a booking for a workshop or lecture, or negotiating a better rate with a supplier.

Your business is dependent on getting enough warm human beings to say 'yes'. Not just the once, but over and over again. And how you conduct yourself is absolutely critical in getting them to a 'yes' decision.

Deadlines, Time Management, Motivation

I nearly missed the deadline for an article once. I stopped to buy a sandwich and check my email, and found to my horror that I had 48 hours to write something for a magazine issue. I then spent the remainder of my journey writing 1000 words in my head, then frantically jotting down my thoughts onto my mobile phone in Tesco's car park before doing the shopping for the evening meal. Time is such a mercurial commodity and in a world increasingly dominated by (allegedly) time-saving technology it seems, paradoxically, to pass ever more swiftly. Now admittedly in my case, along with the loss of hair, this may be a function of age. I would however assert that many of the devices we use to manage our time end up having the opposite effect. I watched a charming documentary about Warren Buffett the American billionaire hoping for clues, I guess, as to how to make my first million – only to be horrified to find that Warren carries constantly in his head a tally of the number of days and hours of life he has remaining in which to achieve his life's ambitions. As a coach, I actively encourage people to set smart goals that have clear dates and times for completion – but running a countdown to eternity seems a little extreme even to me! And so to the reasoning behind this chapter. How can we manage time in simple and elegant ways? Why, despite our best efforts, do we let our personal deadlines slip – or fail to set any goals to start with? Let's have a look at a variety of things that help and hinder our relationship with time.

Prioritising unpleasant tasks

The knowledge that something unpleasant has to be done can really slow you down. It lingers much too long on the 'Things to Do' list and saps your energy. It hangs around like a bad smell and pollutes your ability to get on with the more exciting stuff. There is only one solution – get the bad stuff out of the way as quickly as possible. I strongly recommend that as part of your daily routine you set aside time and work on these tasks exclusively until they are done. What is it you hate and continually put off doing? Identify it and eliminate it as soon as possible and you'll feel much better.

Beware lists

Lists are thoroughly necessary and we all use them, but how many tasks creep from one day's list to the next and remain undone? Listing encourages us to fool ourselves into thinking that something is being done. I've found myself being asked why something has not happened, and I say, "'yes I know – but it's on my list!" Maybe there are ways to manage your tasks more actively.

On extremely busy days I write each task from my list onto a separate post-it note and stick them all on my desk. I write the amount of time I estimate each task will take in the top right hand corner of each post-it, and arrange them in the order that I intend to tackle them. I then take great pleasure in trying to 'beat the clock' rewarding myself by scrunching up and binning each post-it when the task is completed, and rewarding myself for any time I have saved with a walk in the garden or an extra cup of tea. The side effect is that I usually win a little time each day between tasks, and it feels like a bonus.

Why does this work for me? Well, there is a good reason for this. We all have a dominant sense – some of us are visual and like things in pictorial or visual form, some are auditory and like text or audio based things, and some are kinaesthetic – preferring some kind of physical activity or involvement within their activities – I'm a bit visual and a bit kinaesthetic – I like the post-its (visual) and the pleasure that comes with scrunching up the task when it is complete (kinaesthetic). What's your sensory preference, and how can that knowledge help you figure out the right time management technique for you? For example:

● You can get great applications for smartphones now that let you make your lists in colour, and set the most important tasks to blink at you until they are done and erased.

- If you hate writing, voice recognition software lets you dictate text straight into your computer (it's actually really accurate) while you stroll around wearing a wireless microphone headset.

- You can download mind-mapping software that lets you organise ideas in thought bubbles visually on your computer screen.

- Or you can employ old technology and stick post-its on the wall.

It's all about finding a technique that suits your values and personality.

Baby steps or big leaps?

At the end of the Second World War a lot of thought was given as to how the restructuring of manufacturing industry might be approached. A lot of the really effective management techniques that are used today evolved out of that process. Amongst them came a realisation that some things are best achieved in baby steps over a long period of time, and some by taking massive, decisive action – getting the change over with and new systems in place as rapidly as possible. Think about the things you want to tackle over the next year – are they best approached with a small step strategy or massive action?

A bit of psychology

There's no point in having goals unless you do something about them. The most important thing is to make the decision to act, and then to carry out the requisite action. Otherwise all your planning is simply 'wish-listing'.

If there's something you want to achieve and it's not happening, you need to know why. Most often, things don't happen because they conflict with your values at quite a deep level.

Your values are the energy behind your goals

Some days you feel that everything is going right, work flows effortlessly, and your creative juices bubble away inside you. Sometimes you end up doing stuff that just plain feels wrong. Getting up and going to work feels like a drag, and there's no pleasure in the work itself. The sense of flow comes when your goals are fully congruent with your personal values. If things aren't flowing, sometimes what you are doing has got out of kilter with your innermost sense of what's important. For example:

● A client wants you to make more of a product that you don't feel excited about any more.

● You've got to do your accounts and you'd rather be making things.

● Income requirements rob you of the time to experiment with new ideas.

Any scenario of this type can rob you of energy and motivation – the trick is to recognise what's happening and find a way around it.

Delegation

Frankly, it's impossible to do everything yourself. Certainly, it's impossible to do everything yourself and do it well. I do wonder sometimes, when I hear of people spending hours filling in their tax forms and doing all the calculations of what they are eligible to claim for against tax – how much creative work could they get done in that time? And how much would that have earned them?

I think you need to do that quick calculation in your head, because if you could be earning more, enjoying life more and being in the flow more from doing the creative stuff and giving the book-keeping to someone else to do, then surely you are going to be a happier being. Now, I know the counter-argument to this – it's well-rehearsed. You are working on your own and you can't afford to pay somebody else to do it. Well, look at the calculation again. Is that strictly true?

Once you get the momentum going and you get extra time to spend on your creative output, is it still true that you can't afford to pay somebody else to do it?

The first thing you need to do is have a think about what you can split off. There will be simple tasks that you can hive off. Someone could do the filing, or book-keeping, or they could sit with you for an hour a week and help you stay on top of your diary and to do list. There are a gazillion ways that you can get help.

You don't have to hire somebody full-time; you don't even have to hire somebody part-time. There are lots of people out there that only really want two or three hours paid work a week. Whenever I've had a problem like this I've just put a message out on Facebook, or I've spoken to a few good friends and it hasn't taken long to find somebody that can help out.

If the notion of a 'Person Friday' appeals you need to be creative in the way you think about it. If you've got a reasonable amount of stuff that you need help with on a regular basis it may well be worth considering hiring a virtual assistant. They are people who specialise in working with small business owners like you. They are often people who have huge amount of expertise in marketing, copywriting or in managing email and databases. A quick search for virtual assistants on the Internet will generate a good list for you to choose from. However, ask around first – it's more than likely that someone you know has one and can pass the details on to you.

The other option that can be fruitful is to go to the volunteering department of your local university and ask if they have anyone who might be interested in work experience and who might take on your research or mailings for you for a small fee. They need the work, but more importantly they need useful, interesting experience to put on their CV.

Please don't dismiss delegation just because you think you can't afford it, or because you don't think you can let go of things in that way. Because generally speaking, most often, you can.

Getting Through Hard Times 19

Some time ago, one of my clients cancelled some work. They simply couldn't afford to carry on with it at the moment. As it was a sizeable contract, I naturally felt a strong mix of sympathy for them and frustration about the knock on effect that it might have on my own cash flow. I'd have to cut my cloth somewhere to compensate.

I didn't react to the client straight away, and after a fretful night, decided to do two things – first to contact the client and make sure that she knew that our working relationship would not be in jeopardy, and second, knuckle down to the task of finding work of a similar value to fill the gap.

I recalled a lesson someone taught me about how the way we react to things is key to our success. The premise is this: 90% of the things that happen to us are (largely speaking) out of our control. How we react - with grace and fortitude, with ill-tempered venom, or for most of us, with something fuzzy in between - can change our fortunes significantly.

Recessions don't last forever. I started my business in 1984 and have had some hairy times, but I'm still here.

I find the trick to getting through the bad times is combination of Buddha like acceptance, making sure I have some huge goal in mind to keep me focussed on the future, and a survival plan with clear targets attached to it.

Here are a few questions people regularly ask me:

It just seems to be one bit of bad news after another at the moment - how am I supposed to stay optimistic about the future?

Don't let yourself be hypnotised by the media. It's much too easy to get carried along on a wave of pessimism. Rise above it!

I've lost my motivation - it's been dented by the pressure I'm under to stay afloat with reduced income - how can I re-motivate myself?

Think back over your career to date – what were the highlights and why? What made those events special? Make a note of what they were. It's important that you bring all you gained from those situations into your plans for the future.

Can you remember what originally motivated you to start your own business? If that has been obscured by the worry of just keeping going, you need to revisit the things that made you feel good about your business before the problem hit. Think through and reset your original goals.

The trick is to be clear about your long-term goals and

use them to balance out short-term difficulties. Set yourself some really ambitious goals - get into your 'stretch zone'.

What can I do to regain my original passion and drive?

Start thinking beyond whatever is causing the immediate problem - where do you want to be when this is all over? What are the core values that underpin what you do? Your values are the energy behind your goals and whatever happens, they are still going to be your main source of drive and energy.

Use positive language. Talk to people positively - talk about your dreams and intentions - what you can do, rather than what you can't (and who says you can't?). It's all too easy to talk yourself into a falsely bleak view of things.

Think about ways of diversifying. Is there anything new you could be doing for your existing customers? Are you sure you have identified all potential buyers for your current products? You can use a business tool called Ansoff's analysis for this - you can find out about this in the next chapter.

Reframe the situation as an opportunity - what can you innovate, invent? Hard times are a great opportunity to introduce new ideas and cut out dead wood. All the smart thinkers don't talk about the problem but rather about what comes next - how do you want your world to look after the crisis has passed?

I'm simply not as busy as I was – how can I use my time to best advantage?

Move into the 'stretch zone' with your creativity. No-one can take that away from you. Try out all the things you've been dreaming about for a while.

Take some time to think about your skills. Could you be using slack time to develop some new skills? Is it a good time to do that internet course, teaching certificate or PhD you've been promising yourself?

Where can I find support?

Find a buddy - someone in a similar position to keep in touch with for mutual support. Talk through all your options and ideas with them - two brains are much better than one.

If you think you are heading towards financial troubles act quickly - a spot of timely advice might just get you through. Very few people are both great makers and financial experts. Sometimes an accountant or bank manager can suggest work-arounds you hadn't thought of.

Get a mentor or coach - now more than ever this might be a useful strategy.

What if I can't sustain the costs of marketing?

There's an old oriental maxim to 'put out more flags' in times of trouble (this fooled the enemy into thinking new battalions of troops had arrived).

Do a bit of inexpensive do-it-yourself PR instead to raise

your profile. Show up at events, network more, do talks and demonstrations, include friends and family in your mailings. Ask existing clients for referrals.

See if you can identify someone who does something complementary, create a joint marketing campaign and share the publicity costs.

A final word

Do what you can to energise yourself - give yourself rewards for keeping going. If you can't afford big holidays, treat yourself to a weekend or even one night away - there are loads of places that deserve a visit. We recently spent a day and night away in a city close by and found craft outlets galore, great pubs and an awe inspiring cathedral. It's too easy to forget all the good stuff that's on our doorsteps - make the most of it and recharge your batteries.

Staying Ahead of the Game 20

I regularly run 'Creative Strategy' sessions which introduce concepts drawn from the commercial world. These sessions are designed to demystify the 'tools for thinking' that big businesses use and show how they can be used effectively to extend the way that people think about their own enterprises.

I firmly believe that it is possible for you as a creative person to adopt 'business-like' ways of working without compromising your artistic integrity.

Creative people are pretty good at the vision thing – but sometimes fail to set clear goals for themselves. The good news is that there are ways of thinking about the future that allow you to set creative goals and business goals in the same breath – so rather than blocking the creative flow, business goals make sense because they relate to the creative process rather than getting in the way.

All of the tools for thinking in this chapter are simple, straightforward, and can be used straight away. You may wish to arm yourself with paper and pencil and put them to work for yourself.

The 'vision' thing

Vision is a funny old word. For our purposes, it simply means being able to describe where you want to go. In business terms Vision usually has two components – 'hard' or quantifiable targets, and 'soft' targets relating to creativity, attitudes and working relationships. Taking time to map out your vision makes everything else much easier to plan. Here are some examples of soft and hard goals:

'Soft' vision: things to do with creativity, attitudes and relationships

● Improving your creative skills.

● Visiting inspiring places - sharpening and refreshing your thinking.

● Improving your client's experience of working with you.

● Getting better at networking.

● Utilising client feedback more effectively.

● Talking to people more confidently about your work.

● Creating a pack of information to give to satisfied customers, which they can then pass on, thus generating referrals through 'word of mouth'.

Hard: things to do with setting targets that can be measured

● In a year's time I want to be earning XYZ £'s.

- Calculating how many items or sessions you need to sell per month to do that.

- Think about the number of enquiries you need to generate by means of your marketing – to get the number of jobs you want each year.

- Calculating a profitable price for your work, or

- Calculating a profitable daily rate.

- Scheduling visits to exhibitions or trade shows to market your work.

Strategic scope

Strategic scope can be visualised as the pathway or road towards the fulfilment of the vision. Some people operate on a single track, making or doing one type of thing exceptionally well. Some may have three 'lanes' – maybe making small items for impulse buyers, working to commission, and doing part-time teaching. Some people work on multi-lane motorways, picking up and responding to every enquiry that comes in the door. All these approaches have their merits and drawbacks; the trick is to know if you are comfortable with your strategic scope. Just how much can you do well? Take on too much and things start to slip. There are two things that should help determine the breadth of this: your values (the codes you live and work by) and your competencies (skills, knowledge and experience).

Your values

What are the values that underpin your work? It's useful to try and define these by writing them down. For example:

● I feel strongly about working in an environmentally responsible way.

● I am/am not prepared to live on the breadline in order to pursue my creative vision.

● I will/will not make widgets for Nuclear power stations.

● Good design must be a factor in everything I make.

● I see myself as a craftsperson, not a manufacturer.

It's worth remembering that your inbuilt values determine the amount of energy that you have for something. If you don't totally believe in what you're doing, you won't do it to the best of your abilities. Nor will you be inclined to stretch yourself or go the extra mile. What you do and what you believe in must be completely congruent.

Knowing your strengths and weaknesses

In order to play to your strengths you need to have an accurate picture of your current skills and attributes, how you need to develop or upgrade them, and whether or not you need to acquire any new skills or knowledge in order to 'future proof' your practice. There is little point in responding to enquiries if you don't have the core skills to respond to them effectively. On the other hand, consummate skill might be wasted in churning out repeat orders for widgets that could be made more effectively by a machine. So it makes sense to audit your skills from time to time to check that they are matched to your overall strategy. That way you have the choice to limit your offer to things you are truly comfortable with, or make a choice to stretch yourself by acquiring new skills and expanding what you offer.

Checklist

- What are my current skills and abilities?

- What do I need to upgrade?

- What completely new skills could I benefit from developing?

Strategic horizon and product cycles

How often do you sit down and think about how you might need to modify your business in response to a changing marketplace? There are a couple of useful ideas to consider when thinking about this:

Strategic horizon

How far ahead do you need to be thinking? Different industries have very different external pressures in this respect. For example, the people who design the ring tones for mobile phones need to be able to respond incredibly quickly to a teen market that is hungry for the latest tone. Pharmaceutical companies on the other hand are bound by years of lab work, tests, clinical trials and licensing procedures before they can get anything into the marketplace. The questions for you are:

How far ahead do I need to be thinking? How rapidly does the marketplace for my product evolve? Could a change in government affect me? Could a change in the law affect me? Could a change in infrastructure or supply chain affect my business?

If you want to 'future proof' your business, what do you need to be aware of?

Product cycles

Related to the above, every type of thing that we create for the consumption of others has a clearly defined life cycle. Some types of thing simply fade away, some burn out quickly, and some – for better or worse, get resurrected now and again. Your product will also have a life cycle.

● Some are produced over generations, evolving slowly – e.g. bicycles, wrought iron gates, ceramic tableware.

● The demand for some lasts only a decade or so – Video recorders, for example.

● And some, a few months at most – the latest computer games, phone ring tones – things that are designed to evolve and be replaced rapidly.

The question for you is this: do you need to have new

types of product or service in development so that when the demand for one fades, you have something else to replace it?

Thinking about customers, products and services

The last idea I want to introduce is a neat bit of analysis which is based around these four questions:

- What do we **currently** make or do for our **existing** customers ?

- Are there **new** customers who might buy our **existing** products?

- What **new** things could we make or do for our **existing** customers ?

- What completely **new** things can we think of for a completely **new** set of customers?

This is called Ansoff's analysis, and it's worth spending an hour or so drawing a grid onto a large sheet of paper (with each of the four questions in a separate quadrant) and thinking openly and creatively about this. If you involve friends, colleagues and family, it will be even more fruitful.

Build your own creative strategy

To get the most out of this chapter, take some time to think about and jot down your responses to the ideas I have introduced – Vision, Scope, Values and competencies, Strategic horizon, Product cycles, and Ansoff's.

You'll see that the creative and business aspects of your enterprise are clearly linked within each bit of analysis. If you set aside some time to work through each one, it will leave you with a much clearer picture of where you want to go.

Find out more about Ansoff's and other tools and techniques on my blog at www.creativemusings.co.uk

Visual Planning

At some point you will need to prioritise all the things you have to do and set them out in a plan that will help you achieve your goals in manageable steps. Traditional business plans are invaluable, but it can be daunting to leap straight to a written plan, especially if you have never done one before. Even if they contain all the right information, they may not give you a clear enough picture of the order in which things need to happen.

Timelines are a wonderful way to visualise events in chronological order. All you need to create a successful timeline is a large sheet of paper. A flipchart sheet will do, although you can use an unrolled length of lining paper if you are feeling really ambitious.

Arm yourself with a selection of marker pens, and decide how long your timeline will be. This can be drawn on the paper as a straight line or a wiggly path depending how creative you want to be, and marked off in units of time - usually months. The ideal timescale is between six and twelve months. Going beyond eighteen months can get a bit cramped and unwieldy.

I find it helpful to start the process off using post-it notes. Think about all the things you need to do; meetings with people, bits of research, getting postcards made, talking to the bank, visiting shops and retail outlets, setting up your website or blog, arranging insurance, designing and sending your email newsletters, finding premises – only you will know what exactly needs to be done. Then write one clear action per note. Have a think about where each belongs on the timeline, and stick it down. Then you have the opportunity to move things around as you explore which actions and events are dependent on each other. When you have the final arrangement, you can then transfer your commentary onto the line in a more permanent way.

Stick your timeline up on your workshop or office wall. That way you can tinker with it, revisiting the diagram as events unfold and your actual path becomes clearer.

This is an ideal tool for thinking through everything that is involved in planning new projects or events - it's highly involving and supports rapid thought processes.

If you are thinking about talking to someone more experienced, or getting advice from a business advisor, they'll be really impressed if you have prepared a timeline like this as a starting point. If someone asks you for a written plan, this will be a major step towards thinking about that, too.

And Finally... 22

I want to finish with a message of encouragement. Taking the first step to self-employment, however small or part-time that might be, is exciting and challenging and scary in equal measure.

You'll find yourself surrounded by people with differing opinions. Champions who will encourage you to do it, and doubters who will question the risk. The champions will radiate energy and support and will be there for you through the sticky moments, the doubters will drain you and add to your resistance.

Gravitate towards those who support and encourage, and stay away from the doubters if you can - or at least insert some metaphorical earplugs if you can't.

Don't procrastinate. Don't wait for better economic conditions, or for the stock markets to pick up, or until you've got that production process or cake mix just perfect.

Procrastination has a whole armoury at its disposal. If you find yourself with a list of pre-conditions to getting started; when the kids are older, when you've got enough time, when you've got enough cash, please make sure you aren't simply putting it off.

When you finally get started, when you overcome the resistance and the doubters, when you've done the first job and sent out the first invoice or had a wodge of cash put in your hand and had your first satisfied customer say 'Thank you, you've done a great job', or 'Can I have your business card, I need to tell my friend, colleague or boss about you', you'll feel like you've never done before.

And it beats the pants off the 9-5. I promise.

Pete can be contacted at:

www.makeyourcreativitypay.com or why not stay in touch by joining the book group?

www.facebook.com/makeyourcreativitypay

Places to Explore on the Web

These are the places I most commonly turn to when looking for answers, tools or inspiration. All of them are great starting points for wider exploration.

Business and Career resources

www.businesslink.gov.uk

www.creative-choices.co.uk

www.businessballs.com

http://mindtools.com/

www.creativeboom.co.uk

Resources for Creative Thinking

www.inspired-entrepreneur.com

www.lateralaction.com

www.t-shirtsandsuits.com

www.stevenpressfield.com/category/do-the-work/

Social Networking ideas

http://gapingvoid.com/

www.sethgodin.typepad.com/

Website, Blog and Email tools

www.hallam.biz/blog

www.moonfruit.com

www.blogger.com

www.wordpress.com

www.tumblr.com

http://posterous.com/

www.constantcontact.com

www.mailchimp.com

Ebook Publishing tools

www.fastpencil.com

www.lulu.com

www.createspace.com

www.getpublished.tv

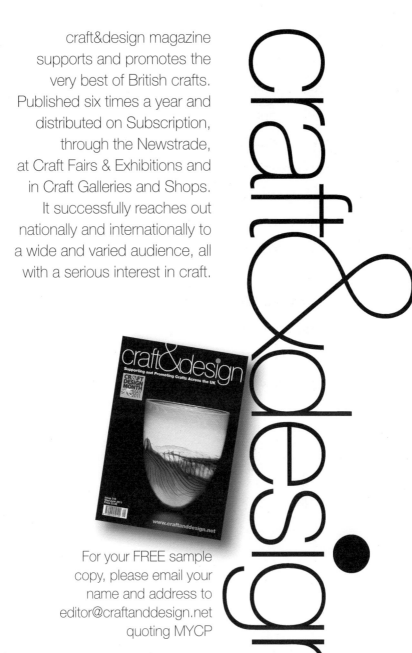

Type set in Myriad Pro 12/17 by
PSB Design & Print Consultants Limited
PO Box 5, Driffield YO25 8JD
Printed and bound in the UK